Retro Stitchery

Oh-So-Cute Embroideries with a Wink to the Past

Beverly McCullough

Martingale
Create with Confidence

Retro Stitchery: Oh-So-Cute Embroideries with a
Wink to the Past
© 2021 by Beverly McCullough

Martingale®
18939 120th Ave. NE, Ste. 101
Bothell, WA 98011-9511 USA
ShopMartingale.com

Printed in Hong Kong
26 25 24 23 22 21   8 7 6 5 4 3 2 1

Library of Congress Cataloging-in-Publication Data is available upon request.

ISBN: 978-1-68356-121-7

MISSION STATEMENT

We empower makers who use fabric and yarn to make life more enjoyable.

CREDITS

**PUBLISHER AND
CHIEF VISIONARY OFFICER**
Jennifer Erbe Keltner

CONTENT DIRECTOR
Karen Costello Soltys

DESIGN MANAGER
Adrienne Smitke

MANAGING EDITOR
Tina Cook

PRODUCTION MANAGER
Regina Girard

**ACQUISITIONS AND
DEVELOPMENT EDITOR**
Laurie Baker

**COVER AND
BOOK DESIGNER**
Mia Mar

COPY EDITOR
Melissa Bryan

PHOTOGRAPHERS
Adam Albright
Brent Kane

SPECIAL THANKS

*Photography for this book was taken at
the home of Libby Warnken in Ankeny, Iowa.*

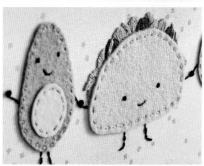

Contents

• •

• • • • Bonus Embroidery Design Online! • • • •
Visit ShopMartingale.com/RetroStitchery
to download Blooming Sneakers for free.

Introduction

• •

I've always been drawn to vintage linens and embroideries. I can't resist rescuing them when I find them in thrift shops and antique stores, and I love using them in my home and repurposing damaged linens into new projects. But embroidery can enhance so much more than simply table linens and pillowcases. I love creating embroidery designs for artwork, home decor, apparel, and more!

The projects in *Retro Stitchery* are fun and colorful, with an updated vintage vibe, and they're great stepping stones to incorporating embroidery and stitching-inspired projects in your home and wardrobe. I give you all the information you need to get started in "Stitching Q&A" on page 6, along with illustrations showing how to work stitches in the "Embroidery Stitch Guide" on page 61, so whether you're a beginner stitcher or have been sewing and embroidering for years, you can dive right in.

The designs can easily be adapted for other projects as well. Maybe you love the design on a hoop-art project but you'd rather have it on a pillow or mini quilt. With the instructions given in "Fun and Creative Finishes" on page 8, you can easily convert the designs to suit your finishing preferences.

I hope you have so much fun stitching and sewing along with me!

~ Beverly

Stitching Q&A

You don't need to have a lot of supplies to start embroidering. In this section, I answer some basic questions that I'm often asked about stitching to help you build your toolbox of knowledge.

what do i stitch on?

I encourage you to be creative with the fabrics you stitch on! You can use quilting cotton, linen, or other similar-weight fabrics for stitching, but there are a lot more options to consider. Denim and canvas work great, and so does felt. I love to use light wool-blend felt for my projects. However, avoid polyester felt because it doesn't hold up well to stitching and you can't iron it.

When selecting fabric, keep in mind that heavier fabrics will require more strands of floss in order for the stitching to stand out, while thinner fabrics usually require a layer of muslin or interfacing behind the fabric to give the stitches stability.

Have fun letting your imagination explore all sorts of materials and surfaces. I've even cross-stitched on caned furniture, a vintage metal colander, and a pegboard!

what supplies do i need?

You can start stitching with just a few notions. Here are the items I've used to create the projects in this book; some are necessary, and some are just items that make things easier.

- **Needles.** Look for a needle with a sharp tip and—because you'll be using multiple strands of floss—a large eye. Embroidery/crewel

needles in sizes 3 to 7 will usually do the trick, but the size needed will normally be determined by the number of strands of floss. I recommend finding something that's easy to hold as well. If you have trouble threading the needle, pick up a needle threader. You'll find it to be super handy!

- **Scissors.** I like to keep a few different sizes of scissors on hand—a large pair for cutting fabric and felt plus a small, sharp pair for quick snips of embroidery thread. I'll also confess to collecting cute embroidery scissors just for fun. That's totally optional, though.

- **Marking pens.** I keep a few different varieties of fine-tip (0.5 mm) pens on hand. Usually, the marks will be covered by the stitching, but if they won't be for some reason, use a fine-tip water- or air-soluble fabric marker. My preferred brand is Sewline. Transfer pens are another option for transferring the pattern. Sublime Stitching makes great fine-tip pens that are ideal for this task. You may find that one pen works better than another on the fabric you've selected to work with, so keep your options open. We'll discuss the transferring process in more detail on page 7.

- **Hoops.** I prefer stitching my projects in a wooden embroidery hoop, but feel free to use a plastic hoop or other stitching frame that holds your fabric taut. If the completed project uses a wooden hoop for finishing, I think it's easier to just use the same hoop for stitching.

- **Rotary cutter, mat, and rulers.** You'll need these items to cut the pieces for sewing projects.

- **Sewing thread.** I use 50-weight Aurifil thread for machine sewing.

- **Floss.** All the projects in the book were made using Aurifil six-strand embroidery floss. I love this brand of floss for its excellent quality and vibrant colors, plus it's wound on wooden spools, which helps to keep the threads tidy and organized. If you prefer DMC floss, I've provided a conversion chart on page 63 for all the floss colors I used in these projects.

how do i transfer the pattern?

This is probably the question I'm asked most about embroidery. There are several methods for transferring the design onto your surface, which I've outlined below. Feel free to use whatever works best for you or for the fabric you're stitching on. I switch between all these methods, depending on the fabric and floss colors I'm using. I also keep a fine-point water-soluble marker on hand for touching up areas that didn't transfer well or for making small adjustments on the design if necessary.

light-source method

Tape the pattern to a window or light box, and then tape the fabric in place over the pattern. Trace the design with your preferred marking pen.

iron-on transfer pen method

For this method, you'll need to make a reverse image of the pattern. The easiest way to do this is to photocopy the pattern from the book using the reverse-image feature on the copy machine, and then go over the lines with a transfer pen. Alternatively, you can make a regular copy of the pattern, and then turn the paper over and trace the pattern onto the blank side of the sheet using a transfer pen. Place the marked pattern on the fabric with the transfer side next to the fabric. Follow the manufacturer's instructions to iron the design onto the fabric. This makes a very thin line that is permanent.

Transfer the pattern to the right side of the background fabric using your preferred method, and then secure the fabric between the hoop rings. A strong magnetic needle minder keeps your needle easy to find. You can find a fun assortment of needle minder styles in my shop at FlamingoToesShop.com.

transfer-paper method

Transfer paper, also called tracing paper or dressmaker's carbon paper, comes in several different colors. Select a color that will show up on your fabric, and before you trace the design, make sure the marks are easy to remove from the fabric you're using. This method works great on darker fabrics or when you don't have a light source or iron available.

Place the fabric right side up on a table or other hard surface. Lay a piece of transfer paper over the fabric, with the color side against the fabric. Then place the pattern right side up over the paper. Using a mechanical pencil with 0.5 mm or 0.7 mm lead, trace the pattern. The tracing paper will transfer the design onto the fabric.

Fun and Creative Finishes

The options for finishing embroidery projects are unlimited. You can use embroidery in quilt projects, for home decor such as pillows and dish towels, and as artwork, displayed in either hoops or frames. Here are some quick tips about different ways to finish your projects.

hoop it up!

Displaying embroidered designs in a hoop is a very popular decorating choice and it's easy to do.

1 Make sure your design is centered in the hoop and the fabric is taut but not pulled so tight that the design becomes distorted. If you need to press your fabric and recenter the design, do it now.

2 Once the embroidery is in the hoop how you like it, trim the excess fabric extending outside the inner ring of the hoop to about ½". Turn the excess under and glue it to the inside of the inner hoop. I use hot glue for this, but feel free to use whatever glue you'd like. Make sure the trimmed fabric doesn't touch the back of the embroidered design or it could distort the surface.

3 If you're adding trim to the edge of the hoop, glue the trim to the back of the wood hoop with the trim extending past the edge of the outer hoop. See the photo of the #tacotrio trim on page 54 for reference.

4 You can also stain or paint the hoop, or wrap the outer hoop with strips of fabric that coordinate with your embroidery, as I did with Choose Joy shown on page 32.

5 Finish the back of the hoop by cutting a piece of wool felt or scrapbook paper the size of the hoop and gluing it to the back of the outer ring. This is also a great place for a label or note if you'd like to sign and date your work.

frame game

1 When framing a piece of embroidery, I usually remove the glass from the frame to allow the texture of the stitches to be more visible. After pressing your design, back it with a piece of fusible fleece or very lightweight batting so that the threads on the wrong side of the design don't cause bumps or ridges when the piece is displayed.

2 Following the manufacturer's instructions, lay the backed stitchery over a piece of self-stick mounting board, or spray a piece of foam core board with basting spray or lightweight glue and finger press the embroidery in place.

3 Fold the fabric edges nice and tight around the board, and then glue the excess to the back of the board, mitering and trimming the fabric at the corners as needed to reduce bulk.

4 Place the embroidery in the frame.

pressing your design

For any project that won't be left in the hoop in which it was embroidered, you'll need to press the creases left by the hoop. To press the design without damaging your stitches, place the embroidered piece right side down on a soft surface like a towel or a wool pressing mat. You want to press on a surface that will allow the stitches to have some give and not be flattened. Press the design carefully, and avoid dragging the iron across the back of the project so that you don't catch any threads or distort the design. The exception to this is projects with woven wheel roses. In those situations, I recommend keeping the design right side up and pressing around the roses as best you can. A mini iron helps reach spots that a larger iron can't.

Happy Stitching!

Hang this stitched saying wherever your happy place is! Whether you're gathering with loved ones in the family room, stitching up a storm in your sewing room, or relaxing in your camper, this framed piece says it all.

Framed Embroidery: 8" × 10"

materials

- 12" × 14" rectangle of white tone-on-tone fabric for background
- 9" × 11" rectangle of fusible fleece or lightweight batting
- 8" × 10" rectangle of self-stick mounting board
- 8" × 10" frame
- Craft glue

embroidery floss

Colors listed below are for Aurifil six-strand embroidery floss. For DMC equivalents, see page 63.

Light Jade (1148) for "This" and "Place" lettering

Spun Gold (2134) for decorative scrolls on sides

Peachy Pink (2435) for "is my" lettering and flowers

Light Emerald (2860) for scalloped lines and greenery

Medium Red (5002) for "Happy" lettering and French knots

embroidering the design

1 Referring to "Stitching Q&A" on page 6 and using the pattern on page 13, center and transfer the design onto the white fabric.

2 Embroider the design, referring to the embroidery floss list on page 11 for color placement, the embroidery key near the pattern, and "Embroidery Stitch Guide" on page 61. Use three strands of floss for all stitching.

finishing

Refer to "Frame Game" on page 8 to frame the stitched piece.

floss finesse

If you're using bold floss colors and light fabric like my version, be careful not to travel too far with the floss on the back of the piece. Although it takes a little extra time to start and end, the results are worth it. You don't want the floss on the back to show through to the front.

THIS is my Happy PLACE

Embroidery Key

—— Backstitch

------ Chain stitch

• French knot

▨ Layered backstitch

◠ Lazy daisy

There's No Place Like Home

Show off your love of home with a cozy pillow. Easily personalized just by changing the color of the fabric and threads, this project would make a perfect housewarming gift.

Finished Pillow: 12" × 20"

materials

Yardage is based on 42"-wide fabric.

- ⅜ yard of white print for embroidery background
- 28 squares, 2½" × 2½", of assorted prints for border
- ½ yard of coordinating fabric for backing
- 12½" × 20½" rectangle of fusible fleece or batting
- 2 yards of white pom-pom trim
- 12" × 20" pillow form

embroidery floss

Colors listed below are for Aurifil six-strand embroidery floss. For DMC equivalents, see page 63.

Dark Grey (1246) for flower center

Dark Grey Blue (1248) for "h," "m," and "e" lettering

Baby Pink (2423) for center of flower petals

Blossom Pink (2530) for edges of flower petals

cutting

From the white print, cut:
1 rectangle, 10" × 18"

From the backing fabric, cut:
2 rectangles, 12½" × 14"

assembling the pillow

Sew with a ¼" seam allowance. Press the seam allowances as indicated by the arrows.

1 Press the embroidered piece and trim it to 8½" × 16½", keeping the design centered.

2 Randomly select four 2½" squares and sew them together in a row to make a side border. The border should measure 2½" × 8½", including seam allowances. Repeat to make a second side border strip. Sew 10 squares together in a row to make the top border, which should measure 2½" × 20½", including seam allowances. Repeat to make the bottom border.

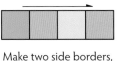

Make two side borders,
2½" × 8½".

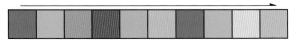

Make two top/bottom borders,
2½" × 20½".

3 Sew the side borders to the left and right sides of the embroidered rectangle. Join the top and bottom borders to the embroidered rectangle. The pillow top should measure 12½" × 20½", including seam allowances.

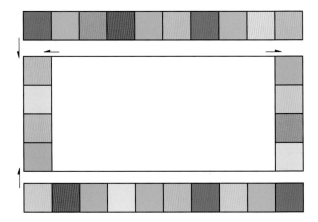

embroidering the design

1 Referring to "Stitching Q&A" on page 6 and using the pattern on page 18, transfer the design onto the center of the white fabric.

2 Embroider the design, referring to the embroidery floss list on page 15 for color placement, the embroidery key near the pattern, and "Embroidery Stitch Guide" on page 61. Use three strands of floss for all stitching.

4 Follow the manufacturer's instructions to fuse the fleece or batting to the wrong side of the pillow top. Quilt as desired. The pillow shown was machine quilted with cross-hatching in the center. Using three strands of Blossom Pink embroidery floss, quilt around the pillow-top center, ¼" from the border. Stitch ¼" inside each border square. Press the pillow top.

5 With the header tape of the pom-pom trim aligned with the edges of the pillow top and the pom-poms facing toward the pillow center, baste the trim in place, overlapping the ends about ½".

6 Press under one short end of each backing rectangle ½" twice; sew along the folded edges to create a hem.

Make 2.

7 Place the backing rectangles right sides up, overlapping the hemmed ends to create a 12½" × 20½" rectangle. Baste the overlapped edges together along the top and bottom of the piece.

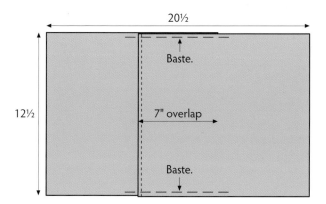

8 Place the pillow top and backing right sides together and sew around all four sides, taking care to not sew over any pom-poms. Trim the corners and turn the pillow cover right side out. Press. Insert the pillow form through the opening in the back.

staying centered

To check the finished size of the embroidered piece before you trim it, measure the size that you need to cut and draw the outline with a water-soluble marker. Make sure you leave the same distance from the embroidery at the top and bottom and the same distance on each side. Once you've marked the outline, you can easily visualize the layout and then double-check your measurements. You don't want to spend all the time embroidering your piece and then have to redo it if you trim the fabric incorrectly. (Ask me how I know!)

Embroidery Key

- French knot
- Layered backstitch
- Satin stitch

Coffee and Tea on the Go

Even your coffee and tea can show off your fun embroidery style with these sweet mug wraps. There's something for everyone here, from a cat silhouette design to a floral teacup. Dress up a travel mug with a wrap and pop in a gift card to your favorite coffee shop for a fabulous gift!

Finished Mug Wrap: 3" × 11", not including ties

materials (for 1 wrap)

- 5" × 14" rectangle of small-scale print for wrap
- 4" × 12" rectangle of coordinating print for lining
- 4" × 12" rectangle of fusible fleece
- ⅔ yard of ribbon for ties OR elastic hair tie and ¾"- to 1"-diameter button
- ½ yard of decorative trim for wrap edges (optional)

embroidery floss (for all wraps)

Colors listed below are for Aurifil six-strand embroidery floss. For DMC equivalents, see page 63.

Light Jade (1148) for outline of teabag

Dark Grey (1246) for staple and string on teabag; "Hot and Strong" lettering; percolator; cat and "Cats, Books & Coffee" lettering; teacup outline, saucer, and side flowers on teacup

Pale Pink (2410) for detail lines and center flower on teacup

Blossom Pink (2530) for flowers on Hot and Strong, "Time for Tea" lettering and flowers on teabag, and "Feeling Perky!" lettering and flower

embroidering the designs

1 Referring to "Stitching Q&A" on page 6 and using the patterns on page 23, transfer the desired design to the center of the front rectangle.

2 Embroider the design, referring to the embroidery floss list on page 19 for color placement, the embroidery key near the pattern, and "Embroidery Stitch Guide" on page 61. Use one strand of floss for the lettering on Cats, Books & Coffee and Time for Tea. Use two strands for all other stitching.

making the wraps

Sew with a ¼" seam allowance.

1 Remove the design from the embroidery hoop and press, referring to "Pressing Your Design" on page 9. Using the pattern, cut out one piece from the embroidered rectangle, keeping the design centered. Also cut one rectangle *each* from the lining rectangle and the fusible fleece.

2 Follow the manufacturer's instructions to fuse the fleece to the wrong side of the front piece.

3 To add trim to your wrap, sew the trim to the right side of the front piece along the top and bottom edges, positioning the trim finished edge so it faces toward the center of the wrap.

4 Choose the type of closure you'd like. If you're using ribbon ties, cut the ribbon in half to make two pieces 12" long. You can trim the ends later if you'd like. Center a ribbon length on each end of the wrap front, aligning the raw edges. The ribbon length should face toward the center of the wrap. Baste the ends in place. If you're using an elastic tie, pinch one end of the tie together and place it on the right side of the wrap

front, centering it on one end. The majority of the tie should face inward toward the center of the wrap, with about ¼" extending past the raw edge. Baste the tie in place by sewing over the piece two or three times.

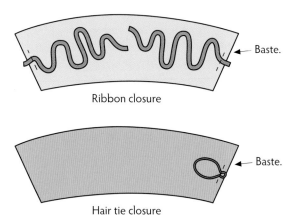

Ribbon closure

Hair tie closure

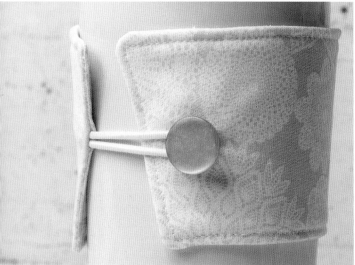

5 Place the front and back wrap pieces right sides together. Tuck any ribbons inside so they don't get caught in the seams. Sew around all four sides, leaving a 3" opening along the bottom edge for turning.

6 Clip the corners and turn the wrap right side out. Use a point turner or similar tool to achieve nice sharp corners. Press, folding the opening seam allowances inside the wrap.

7 Topstitch around the entire wrap ⅛" from the edges, sewing the opening at the bottom closed at the same time.

8 If you're using an elastic hair tie closure, sew the button in the center of the left end of the wrap.

9 Wrap the fabric around your chosen mug and either tie the ribbons or slip the elastic loop over the button to hold the wrap in place.

Embroidery Key

—— Backstitch

• French knot

◗ Lazy daisy

— Straight stitch

¼" seam allowance

Cats, Books, & Coffee

Time for Tea

HOT ❀AND❀ STRONG!

FEELING PERKY!

Tiny Bouquets

Show off your love of embroidery with quick, colorful jewelry.
Mini hoops are the perfect holders for small pieces of stitched art
that are easy to turn into necklaces or brooches–whatever suits
your fancy!

Woven Roses Trio Necklace: 1½" × 1¾"

Daisy Trio Brooch: 1¾" × 2½"

Single Daisy Necklace: 1¾" Diameter

materials (for 1 hoop)

- 5" × 5" piece of light background fabric
- Mini hoop frame kit with opening to fit
  embroidered piece*
- Chain or pin back for finishing
- Craft glue

*The hoops shown are from Artbase, an Etsy shop.

embroidery floss

*Colors listed below are for Aurifil six-strand
embroidery floss. For DMC equivalents, see page 63.*

single daisy necklace

Dark Grey (1246) for flower center

Bright Pink (2425) for center of flower petals

Blossom Pink (2530) for edges of flower petals

woven roses trio necklace

Light Jade (1148) for stems and leaves

Golden Honey (2214) for top flower

Bright Pink (2425) for left flower

Blossom Pink (2530) for right flower

daisy trio brooch

Spun Gold (2134) for flower centers

Peony (2440) for flower petals

Olive Green (5016) for stems and leaves

embroidering the designs

1 Referring to "Stitching Q&A" on page 6 and using the patterns below, transfer the desired floral design onto the fabric square.

2 Using a hoop other than the one in which the finished design will be framed, embroider the selected design, referring to the embroidery floss list on page 25 for color placement, the embroidery key below, and "Embroidery Stitch Guide" on page 61. For the single daisy design, use three strands of floss for all stitching. For the woven roses trio and daisy trio designs, use two strands of floss for all stitching.

finishing

1 Refer to "Hoop It Up!" on page 8 to trim the excess fabric and finish the back of the mini hoop, tightening the screw if necessary. Glue the backing piece in place.

2 Add a necklace chain through the ring at the top center of the hoop, or glue a pin back to the backing piece.

Embroidery Key

— Backstitch

• French knot

⟳ Lazy daisy

▢ Satin stitch

✼ Woven wheel rose

Secret Garden

Create a delightful version of a fairy garden with this Secret Garden cork hoop wreath! The wreath itself is fun to make, but you can be really inventive with what you put in the center as well. The project may look complicated, but construction is actually very simple. After you've made one embroidery hoop wreath, you'll want to make more!

Finished Hoop: 8" Diameter

materials

- 10" × 10" piece of natural stitchable cork*
- 8"-diameter wood embroidery hoop
- 4"-diameter wood embroidery hoop
- Soft moss, assorted artificial mushrooms, and mini foam bird for hoop center
- Water-soluble pen
- Craft glue

The wreath shown is made with DMC cork.

embroidery floss

Colors listed below are for Aurifil six-strand embroidery floss. For DMC equivalents, see page 63.

Spun Gold (2134) for leaves, stems, and large starflowers

Red Wine (2260) for French knot clusters

Light Avocado (2886) for pine needle sprays

Very Dark Grass Green (2890) for large leaf spray and stems for French knot plant

Turf Green (4129) for cypress stems, small leaf spray, and pointed leaf spray

Medium Red (5002) for small French knot flowers and large starflowers

Marine Water (5014) for small leaf sprays and small starflowers

Jedi (6736) for centers of starflowers

embroidering the design

1 Referring to "Stitching Q&A" on page 6 and using the pattern on page 31, transfer the design onto the cork square, but do not transfer the inner-hoop circle line. I found that an iron-on transfer pen worked best for this. Use a pressing cloth when ironing the cork and be careful not to overheat it. When marking the lines for the pine needle sprays, I recommend marking only the stem and the ends of the needle lines. You'll be stitching these with one strand of floss, and it will be hard to cover up marked lines.

2 Place the design in the hoop it will be framed in, making sure the design is centered so you don't have to move it when you're done stitching. Tighten the screw as much as you can to position the cork securely in the hoop.

3 Embroider the design, referring to the embroidery floss list on page 27 for color placement, the embroidery key near the pattern, and "Embroidery Stitch Guide" on page 61. Use two strands of floss to stitch the French knots in the center of the starflowers, one strand of floss for the pine needle leaves, and three strands of floss for all the remaining stitching.

be knotty

I knot and cut the thread after finishing each color section, rather than carrying the thread from one side of the hoop to the other. If the thread crosses the center of the hoop, it will show or need to be cut when the center opening is cut out.

finishing

1 Turn the hoop over so the back faces you. Center just the inner ring of the 4" hoop on the back of the cork. Check your measurements to make sure it's directly in the center. With the water-soluble pen, trace around the inside of the ring. Use sharp embroidery scissors to pierce a hole in the center of the traced circle. Cut approximately 1" inside the traced circle (so that the opening is about a 3" circle, not a 4" circle).

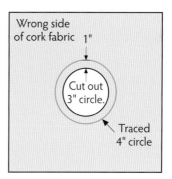

Wrong side of cork fabric 1"

Cut out 3" circle.

Traced 4" circle

2 Clip approximately every ½" from the cut edge to the marked line.

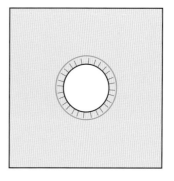

4 Take the screw out of the 4" outer hoop ring. Open up the hoop as much as possible without cracking the wood, and carefully fit it around the inner ring. The clipped cork edges will be between the two hoop rings. Put the screw back in the hoop and tighten the hoop as much as you can. It will be a little tight because it's right up against the back of the cork. Try to tighten the cork as best you can to make sure it looks flat and straight between the two hoops. You can pull on the outer cork and the little cut pieces a bit, but make sure not to pull too hard or you may tear off those little cut pieces.

4" hoop
outer ring

3 Place the inner ring of the 4" hoop under the opening (on the right side). Push the ring into the opening so the circle opens up. The clipped edges will be on the outside of the hoop. Try to center the hoop in the opening as much as possible. If the circle is too tight, make your cuts a little deeper, but do this evenly around the circle so the hoop still sits in the center. Carefully check the inner hoop placement on the front to make sure it looks centered.

5 Refer to "Hoop It Up!" on page 8 to finish the back of the embroidery hoop. Hot glue works great here because cork is stiffer than fabric. Glue the inner cut pieces of cork to the back of the 4" embroidery hoop.

6 Glue moss, mushrooms, and the bird to the inner edges of the small hoop as desired.

4" hoop
inner ring

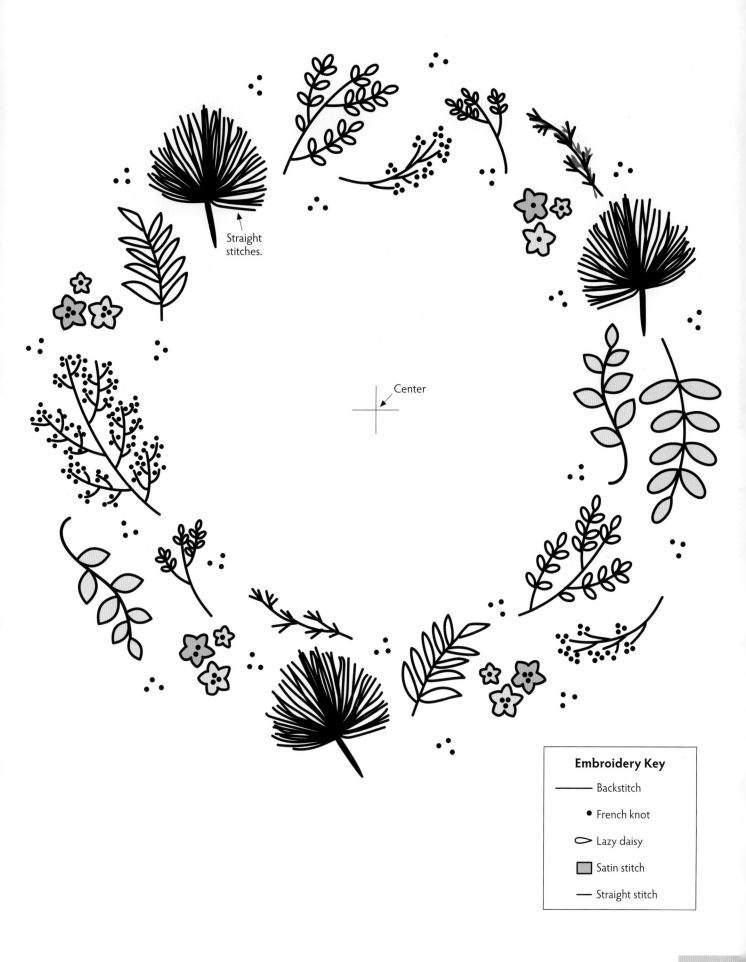

Straight
stitches.

Center

Embroidery Key

——— Backstitch

• French knot

◯ Lazy daisy

▨ Satin stitch

— Straight stitch

Choose Joy

Inspirational projects are so fun to stitch and give as gifts. With all of its cheerful, colorful flowers, this hoop is sure to brighten anyone's day!

Finished Hoop: 8" Diameter

materials

- 11" × 11" square of light blue solid fabric for background
- ⅛ yard of pink print fabric for wrapping hoop
- 8"-diameter wood embroidery hoop
- Craft glue

cutting

From the pink print, cut:
2 strips, 1" × 42"

embroidery floss

Colors listed below are for Aurifil six-strand embroidery floss. For DMC equivalents, see page 63.

Light Jade (1148) for large leaves

Medium Butter (2130) for three small and two large five-petal flowers

Peachy Pink (2435) for three woven wheel roses, five small daisies, one small five-petal flower, and French knot flowers

Steel Blue (2775) for lettering and five small five-petal flowers

Medium Red (5002) for 11 small daisies, two small five-petal flowers, and two woven wheel roses

Marine Water (5014) for small leaves and stems

Sea Biscuit (6722) for flower centers and three small five-petal flowers

embroidering the design

1 Referring to "Stitching Q&A" on page 6 and using the pattern on page 35, transfer the pattern onto the light blue square.

2 Embroider the design, referring to the embroidery floss list on page 33 for color placement, the embroidery key near the pattern, and "Embroidery Stitch Guide" on page 61. Use three strands of floss for all stitching.

finishing

1 Wrap the pink fabric strips around the outer ring of the hoop and glue the ends in place.

2 Refer to "Hoop It Up!" on page 8 to trim the excess fabric and finish the back of the embroidery hoop.

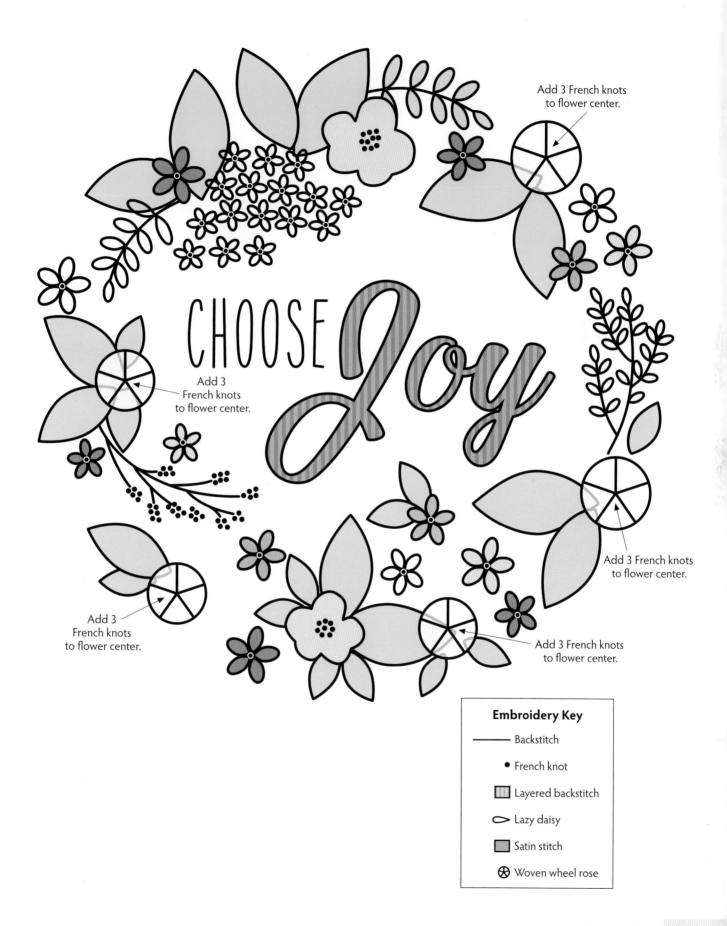

Add 3 French knots to flower center.

Add 3 French knots to flower center.

Add 3 French knots to flower center.

Add 3 French knots to flower center.

Add 3 French knots to flower center.

CHOOSE Joy

Embroidery Key

—— Backstitch

• French knot

Layered backstitch

Lazy daisy

Satin stitch

Woven wheel rose

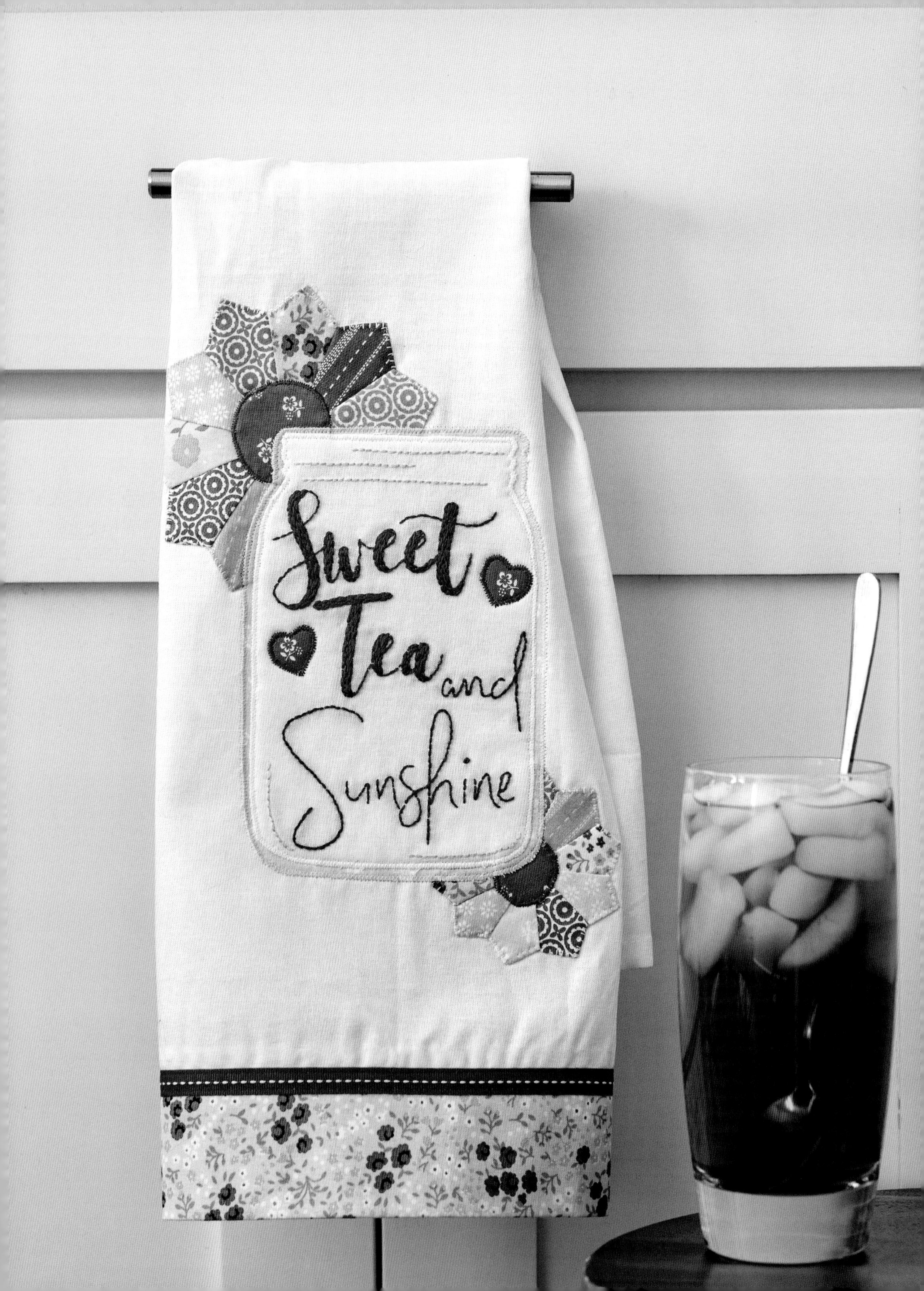
Sweet
Tea and
Sunshine

Summer Days

Pretty, colorful dish towels do so much to brighten up a kitchen and are a simple way to add extra style to your decor, whether they're for function or just for looks! This sweet towel is a great way to use up a few scraps as well.

Finished Dish Towel: 17" × 29"

materials

Yardage is based on 42"-wide fabric.

- ⅝ yard of off-white linen for dish towel and jar appliqué
- 10" × 10" square of aqua solid for jar backing
- Scraps of assorted prints for Dresden wedges
- 6" × 6" square of red print for Dresden circles and hearts
- ¼ yard of aqua print for dish towel band
- ⅔ yard of ¼"- or ⅜"-wide ribbon for band accent
- ½ yard of 17"-wide paper-backed fusible web
- 10" × 10" square of lightweight fusible fleece
- Template plastic

embroidery floss

Colors listed below are for Aurifil six-strand embroidery floss. For DMC equivalents, see page 63.

Lobster Red (2265) for lettering

Light Grey Turquoise (2805) for jar detail lines

cutting

Trace the large and small Dresden wedge patterns on page 40 onto template plastic and cut them out. Use the templates to cut the pieces from the fabrics indicated.

From the off-white linen, cut:
1 rectangle, 18" × 28"
1 square, 8" × 8"

From the assorted scraps, cut:
8 large Dresden wedges
8 small Dresden wedges

From the red print, cut:
1 large Dresden circle
1 small Dresden circle
2 hearts

From the aqua print, cut:
1 strip, 5" × 18"

embroidering the design

1 Referring to "Stitching Q&A" on page 6 and using the pattern on page 40, transfer the jar outline (not the jar backing), jar detail lines, and lettering to the linen 8" square.

2 Embroider the jar detail lines and lettering *only*, referring to the embroidery floss list on page 37 for color placement, the embroidery key near the pattern, and "Embroidery Stitch Guide" on page 61. *Do not embroider the inner jar outline.* Use three strands of floss for all stitching.

making the appliqués

1 Following the jar backing outline, trace one jar, one large circle, one small circle, and two hearts onto the paper side of the fusible web. Roughly cut out each shape. Follow the manufacturer's instructions to iron the circle and heart shapes onto the wrong side of the red print and the jar backing onto the wrong side of the aqua solid. Cut out each shape on the drawn lines.

2 Remove the embroidered jar piece from the hoop. Refer to "Pressing Your Design" on page 9 to press the piece. Follow the manufacturer's instructions to fuse the fleece to the wrong side of the embroidered piece. Cut out the shape on the marked inner jar outline.

3 Fold each large Dresden wedge in half lengthwise, right sides together. Stitch ¼" from the top of the piece. Clip the corners at the fold and turn each piece right side out. Push out the points. Press. Repeat with the small Dresden wedges.

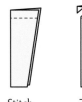

Stitch widest end.   Trim corner.   Make 8.

4 Stitch the eight large Dresden wedges together along their sides. Repeat with the small Dresden wedges.

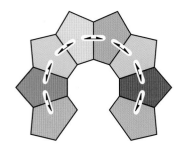

Make one of each Dresden unit.

assembling the dish towel

1 Place the linen 18" × 28" rectangle on your ironing board. Remove the paper backing from all the fusible-web shapes. Center the aqua jar on the rectangle, 3½" from one short end. Referring to the photo on page 36 as needed, tuck the large and small Dresden units under the corners of the jar so the Dresden Plate raw edges are under the fabric. Place the circles over the centers of the Dresden Plates to cover the opening raw edges, tucking them under the jar a little also. Press well so that the fusible-web shapes are holding everything in place.

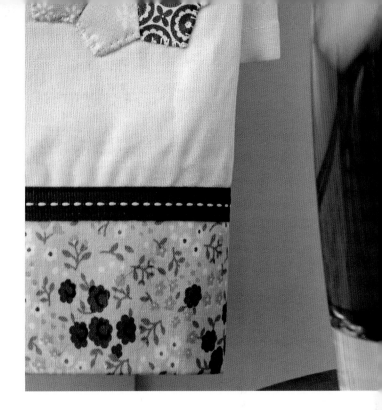

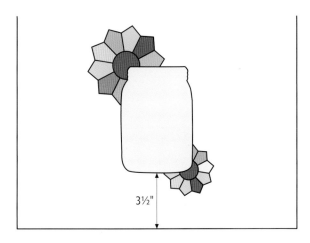

3½"

2 Following the jar outline (not the jar backing), trace one jar onto the paper side of the fusible web. Cut out the shape on the drawn lines. Remove the paper backing and fuse the shape to the fusible-fleece side of the embroidered jar. Remove the remaining paper backing and center the piece over the aqua jar backing. There should be about ⅛" of aqua showing around the entire jar. Fuse the piece in place. Fuse the hearts to the jar where indicated on the pattern.

3 Using a narrow zigzag stitch and matching thread, appliqué the jar, the Dresden Plate center circles, and the hearts in place. Use a blanket stitch and neutral thread to appliqué the Dresden Plates in place.

4 Press the aqua strip in half lengthwise, wrong sides together. With the raw edges aligned and right sides facing, sew the band to the bottom edge of the dish towel using a ½" seam allowance. Serge or zigzag the raw edges. Press the band away from the towel.

5 Center and sew the ribbon over the band seam. Trim the ribbon ends even with the sides of the towel.

6 Press under ¼" twice along the long sides of the towel and then sew close to the fold. To create mitered corners at the top, press the raw edge under ¼" twice. Open up the pressed edge and fold the corners at a 45° angle so the point is aligned with the bottom crease mark. Refold the edge and stitch the hem in place.

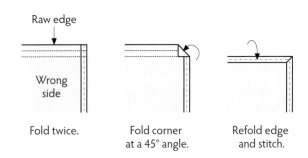

Raw edge

Wrong side

Fold twice.

Fold corner at a 45° angle.

Refold edge and stitch.

Large Dresden wedge
Cut 8 from assorted prints.

Small Dresden wedge
Cut 8 from assorted prints.

Large Dresden circle
Cut 1 from red print.

Small Dresden circle
Cut 1 from red print.

Mason jar

Mason jar backing
Cut 1 from aqua solid.

Heart appliqué placement

Heart
Cut 2 from red print.

Embroidery Key

—— Backstitch

▨ Layered backstitch

Every Day I'm Hustlin'

Display this little art piece in your office or studio—the wrapped canvas is super easy to hang on a wall or display on a shelf, and it provides a fun and different way to show off your stitching.

Finished Piece: 8" × 8"

materials

- 12" x 12" square of aqua print for background
- 10" x 10" square of fusible fleece
- 8" x 8" square canvas-wrapped frame
- Craft glue

embroidery floss

Colors listed below are for Aurifil six-strand embroidery floss. For DMC equivalents, see page 63.

Light Jade (1148) for large leaves and outer leaf circle

Lemon (2115) for two small daisies, one medium flower, and medium woven wheel rose

Orange Mustard (2140) for banner outline and fill, two small daisies, centers of woven wheel roses, centers of small daisies, and center of lemon flower

Red Wine (2260) for three small daisies and two medium flowers

Bright Pink (2425) for outline of banner flowers and large woven wheel rose

Blossom Pink (2530) for inner petals on banner flowers, small woven wheel rose, two small daisies, and centers of medium flowers

Jedi (6736) for lettering and centers of large banner flowers

embroidering the design

1 Referring to "Stitching Q&A" on page 6 and using the pattern on page 43, transfer the design onto the aqua square.

2 Embroider the designs, referring to the embroidery floss list on page 41 for color placement, the embroidery key near the pattern, and "Embroidery Stitch Guide" on page 61. Use three strands of floss for all stitching.

finishing

1 Refer to "Pressing Your Design" on page 9 to press the design. Follow the manufacturer's instructions to center and fuse the fleece to the wrong side of the stitched design.

2 Wrap the fabric around the canvas and glue the top and bottom sides into place, pulling the fabric tight without distorting it. In the same manner, glue the right and left sides into place. Trim the excess fleece at the corners and fold the fabric to create nice square corners around the canvas. Make sure all loose fabric is glued or trimmed on the back of the canvas.

Embroidery Key

—— Backstitch	⌒ Lazy daisy
--- Chain stitch	▨ Satin stitch
• French knot	✳ Woven wheel rose
▦ Layered backstitch	

Add 3 French knots to flower center.

EVERY DAY I'm HUSTLIN'

Add 3 French knots to flower centers.

Let's Get Lost

I'm always up for a travel adventure! My family loves road trips, plane trips ... vacations of any kind. I love to keep all my packing organized with zipper bags, and I firmly believe that you can never have enough of them. This darling bag is just what you need to get ready for the road.

Finished Bag: 6" × 9½"

materials

Yardage is based on 42"-wide fabric.

- 10" × 10" square of light green print for embroidery background
- ⅓ yard of teal floral for accent panel
- ⅓ yard of cream floral for lining
- ⅓ yard of fusible fleece
- 14"-long cream zipper

embroidery floss

Colors listed below are for Aurifil six-strand embroidery floss. For DMC equivalents, see page 63.

Light Jade (1148) for outline of car and windows

Lemon (2115) for medium flower and small daisies

Pale Pink (2410) for medium flower, small daisies, and centers of medium flowers

Blossom Pink (2530) for largest flower, wheel rims, small daisies, and running stitch detail on front of bag

Light Emerald (2860) for leaf sprays and stems of flowers on ground

Medium Red (5002) for medium flower, small daisies, and French knots

Jedi (6736) for lettering, tires, and bumpers

cutting

From the teal floral, cut:
1 rectangle, 4" × 7½"
1 rectangle, 7½" × 10½"

From the cream floral, cut:
2 rectangles, 7½" × 10½"

From the fusible fleece, cut:
2 rectangles, 7½" × 10½"

embroidering the design

1 Referring to "Stitching Q&A" on page 6 and using the pattern on page 47, transfer the design onto the light green square.

2 Embroider the design, referring to the embroidery floss list on page 45 for color placement, the embroidery key near the pattern, and "Embroidery Stitch Guide" on page 61. Use three strands of floss for all stitching.

assembling the bag

Sew with a ½" seam allowance unless otherwise indicated. Press the seam allowances as indicated by the arrows.

1 Trim the embroidered piece to 7½" square, keeping the design centered.

2 Sew the teal 4" × 7½" rectangle to the left edge of the embroidered square. Using three strands of Blossom Pink floss, work a running stitch ¼" from both sides of the seam.

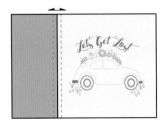

3 Follow the manufacturer's instructions to fuse a fleece rectangle to the wrong side of each cream floral lining rectangle.

4 Open up the zipper and place it on the top edge of the bag front, right sides together, lining up the edge of the zipper with the top of the fabric. Place a lining rectangle over the bag front, right sides together, aligning all of the edges. Using a ¼" seam allowance, sew the top edges together, sewing through all the layers.

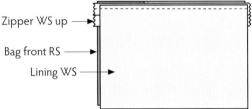

Zipper WS up

Bag front RS

Lining WS

5 Repeat step 3 on the other half of the zipper with the teal 7½" × 10½" rectangle and the remaining lining rectangle to make the bag back. Fold the front and back pieces on each half so they're wrong sides together. Press along the top edges, being careful not to touch the zipper teeth with the iron and melt them.

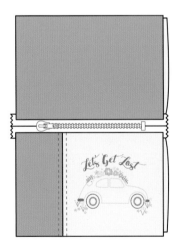

6 Open up the front and back pieces and place them right sides together, with the front and back facing each other, the lining pieces facing each other, and the zipper in the center. Make sure the zipper is still open, and then stitch around all four sides, leaving a 4" opening at the bottom for turning. Partially close the zipper and then cut off the excess zipper tape that extends beyond the bag edges.

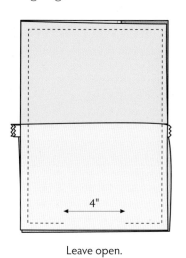

Leave open.

7 Fold each corner of the bag and lining so that the side seams meet the bottom seam. Mark a line 1" down from the corner point and sew across this line. Trim the corner ¼" from the stitching.

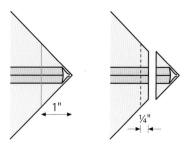

8 Turn the bag right side out through the opening in the lining. Hand sew the opening closed and press the lining. Tuck the lining into the bag and press the bag.

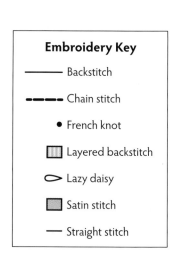

Embroidery Key

—— Backstitch

- - - Chain stitch

• French knot

▊ Layered backstitch

⌒ Lazy daisy

▊ Satin stitch

— Straight stitch

Farmers' Market

Dress up a denim jacket with a retro-inspired design. Florals add color to the back panel, elevating this rugged outdoor classic to chic and feminine. This design would also look fabulous worked in a monochromatic color scheme or an autumn-inspired palette.

materials

- Purchased denim jacket*

If there are seams on the back of your jacket, check to be sure the design fits. You can always remove or add duplicate flowers if you need to adjust the pattern to work with your jacket.

embroidery floss

Colors listed below are for Aurifil six-strand embroidery floss. For DMC equivalents, see page 63.

Light Jade (1148) large leaf sprays and stems and leaves of French knot flower

Dark Grey (1246) for center of yellow and pink ombré flowers

White (2024) for small daisies and base of French knot flower

Lemon (2115) for French knot flower, inner petals of two yellow ombré flowers, and outer petals of one yellow ombré flower

Medium Butter (2130) for outer petals of two yellow ombré flowers and inner petals of one yellow ombré flower

Red (2250) for small daisies and rose details and outer edges

Bright Pink (2425) for fill of lower rose and inner petals of pink ombré flowers

Peachy Pink (2435) for fill of upper rose and outer petals of pink ombré flowers

Mint (2830) for outline and veins of large and small individual leaves and small leaf sprays

Light Emerald (2860) for fill of large and small individual leaves

embroidering the design

1 Referring to "Stitching Q&A" on page 6 and using the pattern on page 51, transfer the design to the center of the jacket back. If your jacket has vertical seams on the back, center the design between the seams.

2 Embroider the design, referring to the embroidery floss list on page 49 for color placement, the embroidery key near the pattern, and "Embroidery Stitch Guide" on page 61. Use three strands of floss for all stitching.

finishing

Once you're finished embroidering the jacket, it's ready to wear. If you'd like to protect the back of your stitching a little more, add a panel of fabric over the threads on the inside of the jacket, cutting the piece large enough that you can stitch the turned-under edges of the panel to the jacket seams. A pretty floral print would be fun and add an unexpected pop of color when you're not wearing the jacket. I also recommend washing the jacket by hand or dry cleaning it to protect your embroidery.

Outline with running stitch and fill with layered backstitch.

Fill flower base with satin stitch.

Stem is two rows of backstitch.

Embroidery Key

—— Backstitch

• French knot

▦ Layered backstitch

⌇ Lazy daisy

- - - Running stitch

▦ Satin stitch

— Straight stitch

#tacotrio

Are tacos a food group? I feel strongly that they should be. It's always time for tacos at my place, and if you feel the same, this is the perfect hoop for you!

Finished Framed Piece: 8" Diameter

materials

- 11" × 11" square of off-white print for background
- 4" × 4" square of olive wool-blend felt for avocado
- 3" × 3" square of light avocado wool-blend felt for seed
- 5" × 5" square of gold wool-blend felt for taco
- 4" × 4" square of kelly green wool-blend felt for lime
- 8"-diameter wood embroidery hoop
- 5" × 5" square of paper-backed fusible web
- 1 yard of 1"-wide fringe trim
- Craft glue

embroidery floss

Colors listed below are for Aurifil six-strand embroidery floss. For DMC equivalents, see page 63.

Spun Gold (2134) for cheese and running stitch around taco

Lobster Red (2265) for tomatoes

Black (2692) for arms, legs, eyes, mouths, and "#tacotrio" lettering

Light Emerald (2860) for lettuce, lime leaves, and running stitch around lime

Olive Green (5016) for running stitch around avocado and seed

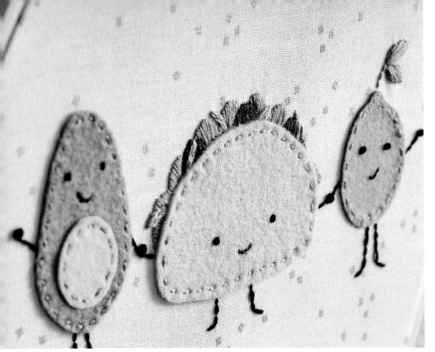

appliquéing and embroidering the design

1   Trace the appliqué patterns on page 55 onto the paper side of the fusible web. Roughly cut around each shape. Follow the manufacturer's instructions to fuse each shape to the wrong side of the appropriate color felt. Cut out each shape on the drawn lines.

2   Referring to "Stitching Q&A" on page 6 and using the embroidery patterns on page 55, transfer the designs for the taco filling, lime leaves, arms and legs, and lettering onto the off-white square.

3   Remove the paper backing from the felt pieces and iron them to the fabric, using the embroidery pattern as a placement guide. If the felt isn't fusing well, turn the background fabric over and press from the wrong side.

4   Transfer the designs for the eyes and smiles onto the felt shapes. You can either draw these on freehand or transfer them with an iron-on transfer pen.

5   Embroider the design, referring to the embroidery floss list on page 53 for color placement, the embroidery key near the pattern, and "Embroidery Stitch Guide" on page 61. Use three strands of floss for all stitching.

finishing

1   Refer to "Hoop It Up!" on page 8 to trim the excess fabric and finish the back of the embroidery hoop.

2   Glue the fringe trim to the back edge of the hoop.

#tacotrio embroidery patterns

#TACOTRIO

Embroidery Key

——— Backstitch

• French knot

– – – Running stitch

▨ Satin stitch

#tacotrio appliqué patterns

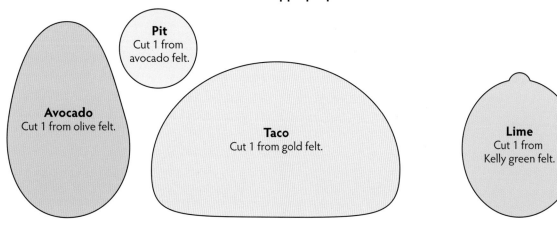

Pit
Cut 1 from
avocado felt.

Avocado
Cut 1 from olive felt.

Taco
Cut 1 from gold felt.

Lime
Cut 1 from
Kelly green felt.

More Tacos, Please!

If you can't eat tacos all the time, the next best thing is wearing a cute smiling taco on your shirt. I love how quick and easy this is to stitch!

Finished Design: 2" × 3"

materials

- Light-colored T-shirt with pocket*
- 5" × 5" square of lightweight sew-in interfacing

The T-shirt can be any color you choose; just adjust the floss colors accordingly.

embroidery floss

Colors listed below are for Aurifil six-strand embroidery floss. For DMC equivalents, see page 63.

Medium Butter (2130) for cheese

Spun Gold (2134) for taco

Lobster Red (2265) for tomatoes

Black (2692) for eyes and mouth

Light Emerald (2860) for lettuce

embroidering the design

1 Referring to "Stitching Q&A" on page 6 and using the pattern on page 55, transfer the design to the left pocket area of the T-shirt, omitting the arms and legs. Check the placement by cutting out the pattern and pinning it in place, then trying on the shirt to see if you like it.

2 Position the lightweight interfacing behind the design on the wrong side of the shirt. Place the shirt and interfacing in the embroidery hoop. Don't pull too much on the T-shirt to make it tight in the hoop; you don't want to stretch out the garment.

3 Make French knots for the eyes and backstitch the remainder of the design, referring to the photo on page 56, the embroidery floss list at left, and "Embroidery Stitch Guide" on page 61. Use three strands of floss for all stitching.

finishing

Remove the shirt from the hoop and trim off the excess interfacing around the taco. Press.

Daily Priorities

Is coffee your creative fuel? Mine too! A great day for me is full of coffee, creating, and sleeping. Hang this fun embroidery in your craft room for a little pick-me-up any time of day, or change things up a bit and use the design as a pillow front.

Finished Framed Piece: 8" × 10"

materials

- 12" × 14" rectangle of gold print for background
- 9" × 11" rectangle of fusible fleece or lightweight batting
- 8" × 10" rectangle of self-stick mounting board
- 8" × 10" frame
- Craft glue

embroidery floss

Colors listed below are for Aurifil six-strand embroidery floss. For DMC equivalents, see page 63.

Light Jade (1148) for leaf sprays, decorative lines, and stars

Red Wine (2260) for hearts, small and large flowers, and French knots

Blossom Pink (2530) for "Coffee" and "Sleep" lettering and centers of large flowers

Steel Blue (2775) for "Create" and "Repeat" lettering and outer lines

embroidering the design

1 Referring to "Stitching Q&A" on page 6 and using the pattern on page 60, transfer the design onto the gold rectangle.

2 Embroider the design, referring to the embroidery floss list at left for color placement, the embroidery key near the pattern, and "Embroidery Stitch Guide" on page 61. Use two strands of floss for the stars and three strands of floss for the rest of the stitching.

finishing

Refer to "Pressing Your Design" on page 9 to press the embroidered piece. Follow the manufacturer's instructions to fuse the fleece rectangle to the wrong side of the embroidered rectangle. Refer to "Frame Game" on page 8 to frame the piece.

Embroidery Key

——— Backstitch   ▥ Layered backstitch

• French knot   ◠ Lazy daisy

Embroidery Stitch Guide

You can do so much with only a few basic embroidery stitches. These stitches will help you create all the projects in the book, plus so much more. Check out my website, FlamingoToes.com, for video stitch tutorials as well!

backstitch

You can create an unlimited number of designs with a backstitch: lettering, flower stems, decorative lines, smiles, and much more. It's the workhorse of embroidery stitches!

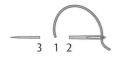

chain stitch

A chain stitch is a fun decorative stitch that is great for outlining and lettering. It makes a slightly thicker line than a backstitch, so it's great for lines that you want to really stand out.

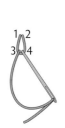

french knot

For years I hated doing French knots! I would fake them by making a bunch of tiny stitches in one place so it looked like a knot. But one day it just clicked, and now they are among my favorite stitches to do! They're perfect for little flowers, eyes, and even to fill in an area for a great textured look.

layered backstitch

This is my favorite stitch for creating thick lettering. Outline the letters with a regular backstitch, and then fill in the open space with more backstitches, offsetting the stitches like bricks.

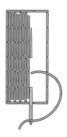

lazy daisy stitch

Lazy daisies are perfect for little leaves and petals of flowers.

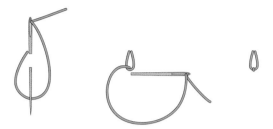

running stitch

The running stitch is so simple and easy, it's my favorite way to add just a little embroidery detail to quilting and sewing projects. It's perfect for adding a bit of color around a seam or making an element in a quilt stand out.

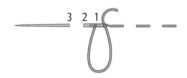

satin stitch

There's something so luxurious about a satin stitch! I love the look of an area filled entirely with pretty, straight stitches. In this book you'll find the stitch used for flowers and leaves.

straight stitch

I use straight stitches most often when I need a nice straight line that isn't very long. It works great for simple flower stems, whiskers on cats, that sort of thing.

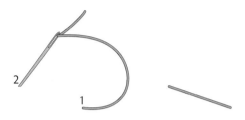

woven wheel rose

This showy flower is surprisingly easy to create. It does use up a lot of embroidery floss, but the finished flower is so worth it!

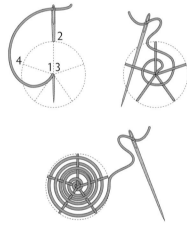

Weave tightly
for best effect.

Embroidery Floss
Color Conversion Chart

· ·

Aurifil Color Name	Aurifil Color Number	DMC Equivalent
Light Jade	1148	958
Dark Grey	1246	413
Dark Grey Blue	1248	161
White	2024	316
Lemon	2115	445
Medium Butter	2130	745
Spun Gold	2134	676
Orange Mustard	2140	972
Golden Honey	2214	854
Red	2250	666
Red Wine	2260	304
Lobster Red	2265	349
Pale Pink	2410	819
Baby Pink	2423	818
Bright Pink	2425	3326
Peachy Pink	2435	760

Aurifil Color Name	Aurifil Color Number	DMC Equivalent
Peony	2440	819
Blossom Pink	2530	602
Black	2692	310
Steel Blue	2775	322
Light Grey Turquoise	2805	3766
Mint	2830	966
Light Emerald	2860	913
Light Avocado	2886	772
Very Dark Grass Green	2890	367
Turf Green	4129	561
Medium Red	5002	3705
Marine Water	5014	817
Olive Green	5016	469
Jedi	6736	317
Sea Biscuit	6722	Ecru

About the Author

Beverly McCullough grew up in a creative family of artists and seamstresses, so it's no surprise that she loves to create! She began sewing and doing needlework as a teenager and made her own clothes and room decor even then. That love for sewing and crafting has grown to include quilting, as well as pattern and fabric design. Her blog, Flamingo Toes, was born out of a love of sharing those projects. Her style could probably best be described as a cross between modern and vintage—she loves taking old styles and making them new and fun again. Beverly is married to her high school sweetheart and lives near Nashville, Tennessee.